BECOME A NOTARY PUBLIC
IN LOUISIANA

BECOME A NOTARY PUBLIC IN LOUISIANA

Process and Possibilities

Steven Alan Childress

qp

QUID PRO BOOKS

New Orleans, Louisiana

Published in 2021 by Quid Pro Books, in the trade paperback edition.

ISBN 978-1-61027-442-5 (trade pbk.)
ISBN 978-1-61027-441-8 (mass mkt. pbk.)
ISBN 978-1-61027-440-1 (ePUB)

QUID PRO BOOKS
5860 Citrus Blvd., Suite D-101
New Orleans, Louisiana 70123
www.quidprobooks.com

This information is provided to aid comprehension of notary practice and procedure, and of the Louisiana notary examination and its official study guide, and should not be construed as legal advice or the practice of law. Please consult an attorney for inquiries regarding legal matters. All information is current as of the date of this printing but should continue to be accurate for the foreseeable future. For information on how to contact the author about this guide, see the *About the Author* section at the end of the book.

Publisher's Cataloging-in-Publication

Childress, Steven Alan.

   Become a Notary Public in Louisiana: Process and Possibilities / Steven Alan Childress.

      p. cm.

   Series: *Self-Study Sherpa Series*, #5

I. Notaries. 2. Notaries—United States. 3. Notaries—Louisiana. 4. Notaries—Louisiana—Handbooks, Manuals, etc. I. Title. II. Series.

KF8797 .C19 2021   2021497529

Cover design copyright © 2021 by Quid Pro, LLC. The Self-Study Sherpa Series image of the munching mountain goat, Sherpa, is a trademark of Quid Pro, LLC, with original artwork © by Mary Ruth Pruitt, used by permission and with the thanks of the publisher.

Second trade paperback printing: August, 2021.

Contents

BECOME A NOTARY PUBLIC IN LOUISIANA

1

INTRODUCTION

This book is designed to be helpful if you're in the beginning stages of becoming a notary public in Louisiana—or just considering joining the profession. It's about the process of registering to be a notary, and why you'd want to. It's about the options, classes, and resources available out there to prepare for the difficult state notary exam. It's *not* a study guide to the exam itself, although we certainly do explain the format of the exam and the structure of the questions so that a candidate knows how to start studying.

There are plenty of resources available to help you prepare for the exam once you've registered, many discussed in our ch. 11. In particular, I've written two books for that next step: the *Sidepiece* that is all about the exam and de-coding the state's study guide, and a *Sample Questions and Answers* book offering practice exams and explanations of what's right and wrong. These books are explained further inside, along with aids and classes available from many sources.

Yet no one had offered a guide to the preliminary but confusing steps you take to be eligible for the exam—or rules and tips you'd want to know right away about the exam process and its "open book." We saw there was a need for such a guide, despite the Secretary of State's website, because the same questions kept popping up over and over with my students the first week of class and on Facebook study groups. This book has what they don't tell you on the website—or what isn't so clear there—about the process of becoming a notary public in Louisiana.

This book is about "what I wish someone told me from Day One when I was thinking about becoming a notary in Louisiana."

So, there won't be details inside *this* book about notary law as such, or explanations of unclear parts of the state's official study guide, called *Fundamentals of Louisiana Notarial Law and Practice*. If you've already ordered that book and registered for the state exam, you're halfway past the level of this guide. Still, many people find the process of getting to that step to be mystifying, and want to be sure they start to prepare for the exam correctly—in a way that doesn't cause problems when they do take the exam. They want to know what comes next after registering. For example, even the rules about inserting notes into the state study guide, and tabbing it, are odd and strictly enforced (ch. 7). You'd want to know before you start *preparing* for the exam what you can and cannot have with you the *day* of the exam (ch. 10), as well as what the exam looks like (ch. 8). And registrants must decide if a class is right for them, and if they should take one in-person or remotely (ch. 11).

This book wouldn't be necessary if the online information about signing up and studying for the exam were a bit clearer, and disclosed some legendary truths about it. We hope to fill a void about the process, rules, and realities of the pathway to becoming a notary in this state. The only pathway—short of going to law school and passing the bar exam[1]—is to register for and take the state-wide notary exam, administered for the Secretary of State's notary division by LSU's office of testing and evaluation. They make it a hard test.

Becoming a notary in Arizona, Ohio, or Vermont

In *any* other state it'd be a piece of cake. You'd take a quick class (if you take a class at all), maybe in a hotel conference room near the airport. Then you'd sit for a relatively easy exam—often simply administered then, at the end of the class. You'd hold a notary stamp in your hands within a few weeks, at most.

But no: *you're* in Louisiana. Don't count on such a streamlined and inexpensive approach to becoming a notary public.

Why you're happy the test covers so much Louisiana law

The huge upside of living in Louisiana is that the civil law notary can actually do powerful and unique things with their notarial commission. In other states, based on the common law, they perform pretty much one function: attesting to the signature. They make sure that forms and legal documents got signed in front of the notary, with proper ID. In many ways they're really just a bouncer!

The Louisiana notary certainly does that function, and often many times a day (charging each time). But in this state, because of the civil law tradition unique among the U.S. states, notaries can perform far more legal actions than just check ID and watch a form get signed—and charge even more for such complicated legal actions.

You can create affidavits, donations of property, and powers of attorney.

You can close house sales, finalize refi's, and draft leases and mortgage documents. You'll file land records with the parish clerk of court. You can turn property into "usufructs" and "naked owners," and make inside jokes about such civil law terms.

You can perform certain adoptions, emancipations, and disavowals of paternity—and help a client appoint a guardian for their kids.

You'll transfer titles and create bills of sale for cars, boats, trailers, and campers.

You'll even write a will or create a trust for clients—without involving a lawyer.

---

[1] In Louisiana, most notaries are members of the bar who receive their notarial commission as a matter of courtesy, taking their oath after they get their law license. This book is not directed at lawyers or law students (where I focus most of my teaching, in fact) but is about the unique but still common process in the state by which non-lawyers—perhaps without college training and no class required—may become commissioned to offer notary services like lawyers. Keep in mind, though, that our law schools don't really teach notary practice, so after you've passed the exam and receive your commission, you can be proud that you're better prepared to perform these important functions than most new attorneys are!

If you did any of those things in any other state without a law license you'd be committing the illegal practice of law. But in Louisiana, non-lawyer notaries are respected professionals who are entrusted with crucial legal actions involving people, families, and valuable property. You can provide great help to clients—or cause Loki-level problems for them if you screw up. That's why the exam has to be so hard. (And for some reason, the very process of being eligible to take the exam is hard, too.)

How hard?

Over the past five or six years, it's a pretty consistent 17 to 23% pass rate even as the number of exams per year increased and the format became open-book and all multiple choice. (Be thankful it's not December 2010, when 14 of 602 takers state-wide became notaries: 2%!?). But even if this typically works out in recent years to about a 20% pass rate, there was even one administration in 2021—the March 13 exam—in which less than 6% passed (19 out of 326). That seems atypical, however, and it was followed by one with a 23% rate.

The bare numbers may scare you off from the whole process before you invest time and money. I hope they don't, because for many people it's worth it, to qualify for a new, interesting profession worthy of pride and profit. There are some ways to look at this pass rate that make it less daunting than it appears, a perspective discussed in our ch. 9. But one thing this book will do that the Secretary of State's info doesn't always do is let you enter the process with eyes wide open. They do make these pass rates public, but not obviously accessed on their website unless you happen to know where to look (see "view statistics" link at https://www.sos.la.gov/NotaryAndCertifications/Pages/default.aspx). And it may not be clear from the website how many different steps you have to go through, and how each requires a separate payment to the Secretary of State.

Even though the exam is "open book," as discussed in ch. 7 below, they don't make it any easier by letting you use only a book that is notoriously disorganized and without a subject-matter index in the back. Especially since answers to questions are often found spread over many spots in the study guide, it's important to write an index into it, and expand cross-references. Classes and study aids teach you to index it. Our *Sidepiece* book's detailed contribution to that strategy is noted in ch. 11.

Anyway, if you're considering becoming a Louisiana notary but are not deep into the actual study phase of your prep, this is the book for you. And if you want to figure out how to get to and through that study phase most effectively, read on.

2

WHY BECOME A NOTARY PUBLIC?[2]

To pass the exam, you have to be truly committed to the process. It helps to know in your core why you want to become a notary. The answer shouldn't just be that a boss suggested a raise if you get that commission, or a non-Louisiana company thinks being a notary is no big deal (like it is in their state) and asks you to do it. Or just that it sounds like fun. I think it *is* fun, but that's not enough incentive to study extended hours beyond what is required in a prep course or seems normal for a professional exam.

But I did want to mention that there are many good reasons to become a notary, beyond the obvious job advancement or expanded responsibilities in an existing career. In career terms, another reason is public relations and client (or customer) development for yourself, apart from its positive impact on your specific job status. Having the seal draws people to you, at home or in the office. And those people perceive you, rightly, as a trusted professional for whom they can see future work in other spheres and give referrals to others. Most businesses kill for foot traffic; being known as a notary is a magnet for those feet. And so, for example, offering notary services becomes a neon sign for insurance agents, mortgage brokers, shipping stores, financial services advisers, and consultants.

There are also several new job openings and lateral moves available for those who are commissioned state-wide as a notary, as you'll be. You can find work in real estate, law offices, government positions, automobile transfers and registration, and financial services that were not open to you before. One can strike out on one's own as a notary, not necessarily affiliated with for instance a real estate firm or a public agency, by opening a notary office or a mobile service yourself. Especially when coupled with other self-employment or services, for example a mailbox-shipping store or as a consultant to hospice care and assisted living places, this can be part of making an independent, professional living. (Luckily, it's also a way to earn fees without their being subject to self-employment tax, and isn't a "profession" in the sense of paying a license tax, see study guide p. 45; yet there's no doubt that the work is "professional" in every important way.)

There seems to be clear room in the market for mobile notary services fronted by an effective website using SEO and make transparent pricing quickly available to interested customers. Upfront pricing or fast quotes would draw clients. Perhaps

---

[2] This chapter is adapted from *Louisiana Notary Exam Sidepiece to the 2021 Study Guide: Tips, Index, Forms—Essentials Missing in the Official Book* (© 2021). It's a bit incomplete in that there are many other tasks notaries perform and more ways to imagine making more money doing them. But it does give a flavor for the question many would-be candidates for the exam pose: why do this?

the travel rate-setting on the website could be framed in terms of typical ride-sharing costs, in a way that clients would understand and feel comfortable paying beyond the cost of the notary or drafting service itself. Getting on the lists of various mortgage providers to do closings (often for up to $250 each) is especially worthwhile—as would be offering to draft wills and powers of attorney *en masse* such as holding a "notary Saturday" at an assisted living facility.

More importantly, there are many non-career reasons to set this goal. Pride of accomplishment is real and valid, and a profession is understandably respected; it's not just a job. People have heard how tough the exam is (well, not friends from other states, where notaries are just functionaries). The work itself requires care, precision, and trust. Drafting testaments and powers of attorney for those who need them protects families and finances for many who might not have such an instrument just when they could use it most. You'll do a lot of good. And as with other professions, you can cause a lot of damage if you don't know what you're doing or you act unethically or unprofessionally. See the movie *Body Heat* for the harm one can cause by mis-drafting a will (and because it's a great film), in that case for violating a Florida rule similar to Louisiana's prohibition against substitutions in a testament.

Notaries in *common law* states (and common law countries like England) do require trust in one important way: that the person who's signing is properly identified. That function is performed by Louisiana civil law notaries, too, but they do much more (see p. 54 in the study guide). The origin of the common law notary, beyond the church-witness function stated on p. 19, owes in part also to the need for the king to be sure the people who came before him were verified as who they claimed to be (say, not an assassin). It was a vital function, to be sure, but the identification-specialty this produced, quite unrelated to practice by lawyers then, made the notary in effect the King's Bouncer, as alluded to above.

You'll be more than that. The *civil law* notary grew out of a wider need in society for the verification, creation, and preservation of vital documents related to property ownership and transfers, family matters, and courtroom evidence (see ch. 1 and 3 in the guide). The civil law notary was always connected to law, legal documentation, and proof in ways that make the notary public historically linked to the profession of lawyer. We're not just ID-checkers (though much havoc results from skipping that step!). When you read the first seven chapters of the guide—about the history and functions of the civil law notary and of Louisiana's legal system—the main goal is to learn the terms, rules, and concepts for the exam. But read them with interest for what they say about the proud tradition you'll be joining and your vital place in the legal system.

Also, this is a position that you'll hold for life—all other states limit the term—at least if you report annually to the Secretary of State, stay registered to vote, and don't commit a felony. Plus it's one you can obtain later in life that will retain its value in your senior years. Most people don't go to med school or become CPAs at an age where it still makes sense to become a notary and the barriers to entry are more manageable. You won't need three years of law school or heavy student debt.

Finally, as challenging as the exam is, there's no real limit on how many times you're allowed to take it. You don't want it to be like the bar exam for *My Cousin Vinny* ("Nope, for me, six times was the charm."). But it *can* be. The point is that it's a hard enough exam that there's no shame in failing it, or retaking it. You can go into it with the mindset that the pressure, though real, is mainly internal and not life-altering if more than one time is a charm. No one should *plan* on taking it over—especially if such thoughts tempt you to "wing it" or not do your honest best. But you can certainly note parallels to the CPA process, by which all candidates already know they must pass four separate exams. Even if the notary exam is the "same" exam instead of four separate parts, passing after three administrations is more efficient and doable than what CPAs endure, if they even pass all four the first time. You may feel better about the process of becoming a notary if you think of it *as a process*—and not just an exam.

Take some comfort in the fact that, as uphill as this exam feels, the effort is what *should* be expected of a "public officer" (p. 45 of the study guide) having such responsibilities and impact on people. Thinking "it's unfair this exam's so hard" only makes it harder to take it seriously enough to study each day, take extensive notes in your state study guide, take practice exams, prep for the exam possibly in a class, and even endure the five-hour exam itself.

At the end of it all, it'll be worth it.

3

Basic Eligibility Requirements

The Secretary of State's website (following statutory law in R.S. Title 35) spells out the current criteria to be eligible to qualify—to even be allowed to register and sit for the exam. To become a notary in Louisiana (and remain one), you have to (all of these):

1. **be registered to vote** in the parish for which you will be commissioned (more on that below, but basically your home, not your work parish) ... but this requirement is waived for non-citizen residents

2. **be a resident of Louisiana**, either as a citizen or resident alien ... this means you can't live in Texas near the border and work as a notary in Louisiana (even though such a requirement for lawyers has long been struck down by the U.S. Supreme Court as unconstitutional)

3. **not been convicted of a felony** (either state or federal), unless you have since been pardoned for it ... it would seem expungement or commutation would not be enough, so certainly begin the process of petitioning for a full pardon early if this disqualification applies to you

4. **be able to read, write, speak and be sufficiently knowledgeable of the English language** ... a requirement that seems to be self-evaluated in advance, on the honor system—which makes sense because the test is in English, hard enough that it weeds out anyone not fluent

5. **be 18 or older** ... which rules out Young Sheldon even if he would ace the exam (but anyway he lives in East Texas, so #2 precludes him)

6. **hold a high school diploma,** or a GED equivalency, or a comparable official home-school diploma of completion

These basic criteria are mandatory even to begin the process of "qualification" on the Secretary of State's website. There doesn't seem to be a statutory process or grounds to seek an exemption or waiver, and I doubt anyone in the Secretary of State's notary office would suggest one is even possible.

So, if this list precludes you, short of suing the state over the Louisiana residency requirement (which I think you'd win, but only after years of litigation), you probably should move on to some other career option. Certainly, though, the stark necessity of a pardon for a felony record ought to serve as one of the main supporting reasons the Governor would consider it for you, as opposed to less clear remedies such as commutation. Anyway, if you are a U.S. citizen, be sure you're currently registered to vote (and actively so—beware of purging).

Note that what's missing on the list is any particular coursework beyond the high school education. That's pretty rare for a profession of such trust and responsibility, and gives everyone an opportunity to become a notary without attending a specific school, or one at all. Still, whether you *should* attend a class, in-person or remote, is discussed below in ch. 11.

The website suggests that you will be commissioned in your parish of domicile (your main home parish, e.g., where you vote). What you should also know is that, for those who pass this state-wide exam since 2005, the parish of commission is not limiting in any way. Your *jurisdiction* will be state-wide, meaning you can perform notarial activities in any parish in the state. So, though your parish status is an important legacy of how notaries used to work in the state (when tests were given by each parish and varied widely), it makes little practical difference to you. You should know going into this journey that where you live is a criterion, but notaries who have passed the exam nowadays have state-wide opportunity. If you someday move within the state, you'll need to register your new parish, but it does not affect the jurisdiction of where you can work.

4

APPLICATION TO QUALIFY AND ORDERING THE STUDY GUIDE

"Application to qualify" sounds like it's a very formal step, may take a while, and means a lot after you finish it. It really doesn't, as it just is the SOS's notary division checking to see that you meet the basic criteria listed in the previous chapter. After you "qualify," you're not a notary. You're just eligible to register for the exam (and not really that, even, as there is a pre-assessment test required first, ch. 5). The only "ducks in a row" you need to get, before applying to qualify, are things like having voter registration current in the parish that's also your home ("domicile") and earning a high school diploma or equivalency.

Nowadays the application to qualify is done, really, online. You need to create an account at the Secretary of State's website, which will be used for all sorts of steps and actions. You may already have an account active if you've used the SOS site for other activities, such as an LLC. (With a previous account you may need to get a Notary Access Code from the SOS, at (225) 925-4704, to associate your new notary profile with an existing account using that email as username.)

Using your "full name"

At any rate, create an account carefully, using a legal name and not a nickname or just initials like J.P. Morgan, to save yourself from having to change the name later to conform to statutory requirements that notaries use their full legal name when notarizing legal documents. (You can always change or clarify it later, as when you are getting your commission after passing the exam, though usually name changes have a fee so it's best to start using your "notary name" now.)

But note that under R.S. 35:12, the "full name" you use as a notary doesn't have to include a full middle name if you don't want to. You may want the shortest "full name" that you habitually use, because you'll be handwriting it below your signature repeatedly and may not want to be stuck with a notary name like the painter Diego Rodriguez de Silva y Velazquez. He probably should just use Diego Velazquez. He certainly cannot use D.R. Velazquez, though either Diego R. Velazquez or even D. Rodriguez Velazquez is fine. (So think: Lee Harvey Oswald, Lee H. Oswald, L. Harvey Oswald, or just Lee Oswald are all OK—but not L.H. Oswald or Harvey Oswald. Nor could he use Buddy Oswald even if he was always called that.)

Your notary name will wind up being the one you use on a stamp and embosser, and how you write out your name on all legal instruments before you. (Your *signature*, however, can be anything you do repeatedly and place on file at the time you file for your commission, so don't worry if the way you will sign looks like initials or uses nickname-ish cursive as long as it's what you give as a sample to the SOS. It could be the symbol Prince used to replace his name for a while.) Your SOS notary account will be the one you use to communicate with the SOS and to upload documents.

Notary identification number and application to qualify

The number they assign to you as a candidate for a notary commission ("applicant ID") will become your actual Notary ID Number you use on documents and stamps, too. You may as well know all of this while you create an account.

Once the account is created, that's what you use to "apply to qualify." That's just verifying status questions and parish residency from the list of criteria in our previous chapter. It won't take long—likely far less than a week—for the application to be approved and make you "qualified." The application to qualify costs $35 (plus a $5 processing fee).

Buying the study guide

The website is also where you can order the current version of the official study guide, *Fundamentals of Louisiana Notarial Law and Practice* (the 2021 one has a blue cover). Everyone also calls it "the study guide" because that was actually in the title of it for years and years. It's now about 670 pages and costs $100 (plus a $5 processing fee online). Don't buy a used version from a previous year, for reasons explained in ch. 7. The SOS usually processes the book order fast and uses USPS Priority Mail in-state, so probably you'll get the book in the mail in just two or three days, and often the next day.

You can also buy it directly (and not pay the $5 fee) at 8585 Archives Ave. (the building behind the main Archives), Baton Rouge 70809, at the customer service counter (by 4:30, but they request you drop in no later than 4:00). You can also order it by mail or fax (check or money order, e.g., if you don't have a credit card saved on the account), though this slows down your getting the book. You can use cash at the service counter. If you just want to check it out and not commit to all this, consider that a public library, college library, or law library may carry a copy that you could use temporarily—or even a slightly older version of it (sporting a different-colored cover) that you couldn't use for the exam but would be enough to skim through for you to make sure the material is interesting and understandable to you. Beware Amazon or eBay selling copies that purport to be valid but are from previous years and thus cannot be used for this exam.

One odd thing about the SOS site is that it seems to only do one transaction at a time—and disallows more if an application, upload, or status is still pending somehow. So realize that if you submit the application to qualify online, you won't be able to go right back and order the *Fundamentals* book. Keep this "hold" in mind if you're close to the deadline to register (discussed in ch. 6).

Where errors in the study guide are corrected

Each year, the study guide's authors find "errata" worth correcting for that edition. Sometimes the SOS office will mail a list of these corrections to you. But look for this sheet anyway, as a PDF online linked on the page "Prepare for the Notary Exam." It's usually linked in text right above the large picture of the book's cover (in 2021, the blue cover). On the day of the exam (see our ch. 10), the testing staff will also hand you a copy of it. It won't come as a surprise to you if you've already downloaded it and considered these changes seriously. They're clearly fair game for questions, as most of the corrections are not just typos. In some years they have issued more than one errata sheet, so refer back to the SOS page from time to time and don't assume the one you downloaded first is the only one applicable to you that year.

Service counter or online account?

Many SOS activities can be done at the service counter, not just buying the book. For example, notary documents may be filed in person there. But keep in mind that some aspects of the process still require that you have an account with the SOS, so you may as well do most of them online unless the state office is handy or the processing charges are adding up.

Also, some of the information for forms handled manually is currently inaccurate. For example, the PDF of an application to qualify says the fee is ten bucks less than it is and has a filing deadline that may not match the actual deadlines discussed in ch. 6.

5

PRE-ASSESSMENT EXAMINATION

After your application to qualify is approved (often in a few days or less), the email telling you this will include an applicant ID (eventually becoming your notary number) and a code to allow you to register for a mandatory pre-assessment exam. Once again you register for that step online, using your SOS account, and once again you pay: $30 for the test, and likely a processing fee.

Even though this is called the "Notary Exam Pre-Assessment," it's an exam that has 0.00 to do with notary law and practice. It's just a brief reading comprehension test, all done online and typically in 10 to 15 minutes. They may give you a selection from an essay about bird-watching or the high school musical and then ask a series of multiple choice questions to determine whether you understood what you read. It's pretty simple if you're a careful reader. It can be daunting if you have issues with reading and analyzing statements of fact, which is its point—the whole *Fundamentals* book will read like Greek to you if close reading of text is not your strength. Taking it, and the score you receive, is supposed to lead to self-reflection as to whether this pathway is right for you.

But don't let the pre-assessment exam intimidate you: its score also counts 0.00 toward whether you can take or pass the actual notary exam. Even if you score an E, you'll be allowed to register for the exam. You have to go through this process before you can register, but it's entirely up to you what you do with the information—an A through E score—it generates. Many students report they did fine on the notary exam after booting the pre-assessment. Several have noted that glitches in the online process led to their "failing" it because the exam timed out early or didn't show on their screens the promised drop-down boxes for answers. They just went on to the next step without trying to fix this one (though you could probably call the SOS office and ask them to generate a new link if it truly is a software problem).

Take it, and its results, seriously?

Still, my advice is to set aside some non-distracted time to take it seriously enough that it does what it's supposed to do: start for you the process of deciding whether this road is one you really want to take. As a tool for self-evaluation, it's useful. The actual letter score, they say, should be at least a B to keep you from having serious second thoughts.

However, to me, the letter score is less useful than just honest self-examination of the bigger picture and *history* of your aptitude for reading and multiple choice exams. If you've never been very good at taking tricky exams and reading text closely, you may find the notary exam very hard (even if you get a B on the pre-assessment). If you've always been able to read and process information, and find things in reference books, don't be dissuaded by a poor pre-assessment. It's just one data point. Candor with yourself about long-seen aptitude counts more than one ten-minute quiz. It certainly has nothing to do with the substance and practice of notary law as such.

Receiving pre-assessment results

You should receive your results in a few days or less—and likely no more than a week—in an email from the LSU Office of Testing and Evaluation (look in spam folder, just in case). Then in a day or two, they've passed along the fact that you've taken it to the SOS office, which will then move your account to the next step, allowing registration for the exam.

You only need to take the pre-assessment test once. Sometimes you've already taken it and their online system is telling you to pay and take it again (when, for instance, you did it a year before, failed the actual exam, and are re-registering). It seems like it will not let you register until you do retake it. But don't do that; call the SOS Notary Division, explain you've already taken it, and request they remove the block so you can simply register for the actual exam. At that point you are supposed to be eligible for the notary exam.

The pre-assessment process is, as a technical matter, just a formality. But it does give you some initial feedback that is somewhat relevant to the idea of reading a 670-page book and being tested on its dense, legalistic content. Self-assessment is important, given the difficulty of the actual state-wide notary exam you'll face.

6

REGISTRATION AND DEADLINES

Once the SOS Notary Division has marked your account as ready to register, probably the next day after you hear from LSU, you can submit your registration for the notary exam in your online account. It costs $100 plus a processing fee, paid by the credit card you've saved. Unless there is some formal reason you can't register (you are past a deadline, the exam is full up), it's simple to do so and you'll show as registered almost immediately for the next exam administration date. You will not have any options as to what date you prefer (if they are splitting administrations over several test days, as they did in fall 2020 and winter 2021, and plan to do Sept.-Oct. 2021). You can't specify what test site you want, though they try to assign you to the nearest one. You won't even know until a week or two before the exam which location is yours, if there are multiple locations for that administration. They may also not give you much heads-up as to which specific date you're assigned, if they do split them across a few weeks.

In most years, they have not had to split it across weeks or use any other date than the one posted on the SOS site. But the pandemic and certain weather events made it necessary in 2020-2021 to split a single administration (say, the Sept. 25, 2021 one), to have some candidates take it another date (in this case, Oct. 23). They simply had no room in the sites they had for the number of candidates who registered, or a weather event delayed a planned test date. Keep an eye on the SOS site for announcements of such changes. They say you have to be flexible and ready to change, and that they won't give refunds if you can't make Oct. 23 while expecting to test on Sept. 25. (As the last test of 2021, that also means that there's no rescheduling, and in the next administration—2022— you'd have to use a different study guide.) In any event, only by emails from the SOS and watching the SOS site's announcements will you know for sure how they'll adapt to overflow and postponements from weather or other news events.

A return to four tests a year?

In most years, too, they have four separate administrations, allowing you to take it up to four times using the same study guide. But the normal schedule fell apart in 2020 and 2021 due to weather and pandemic restrictions. They wound up with more actual test dates (different exams given over a few Saturdays) but only two administrations. That sounds like they expanded candidates' opportunities. But a registrant was only allowed to take the exam once an administration (e.g., you couldn't take it both Feb. 27 and Mar. 27), or even choose which day worked best, making the exam only available twice a year for anyone. Let's hope that 2022 will allow a return to one administration each season, allowing you to take it four times that year if necessary (hopefully not). The main problem with having fewer administrations spread out this way was that one could study starting in April for the fall exam, but if they failed it, they'd have to study in a new book for the next time they could take it. All that time marking up one book and not having it for the next time! If they do return to four tests per year, you can register for the present one with confidence there'd be a chance to register again a month later for the next. And there'll be more predictability to the actual date you'd get assigned to take it, weather permitting.[3]

Deadlines

Deadlines matter, so register in plenty of time. As the above suggests, each step may introduce a little delay, and there are more steps than one would think for just getting to the point of being allowed to sit for an exam. They always have the option to limit the number of total test-takers in a sitting (more on that soon), so that's another reason to register as soon as you're committed to taking the exam.

The absolute deadline to register is 30 days before the exam date (meaning the first exam date if there is a series of expected dates for that administration—e.g., Sept. 25, not Oct. 23 for the fall 2021 series). For Sept. 25, the registration deadline is Aug. 26. Before that, the pre-assessment deadline is Aug. 19 (always a week before the registration deadline). In essence, you must begin the process 37 days before the exam date. Waiting till that last minute runs many risks, including the problem with your account being stuck on a pending process (like ordering a book), not allowing you to sign up for pre-assessment; and the risk that all sorts of glitches in the system make you unable to register the last day allowed for that exam. But if it really is the last day for either pre-assessment or exam registration according to the SOS website, be sure not to order a book first. (Realistically you likely need more than five weeks to prepare anyway.)

Different sites, different applicant limits

So far in 2021, the SOS website has not suggested a cap on the absolute number of applicants for the remaining administration. Instead, Oct. 23 acts as a spillover date. Presumably they will make all three of the usual test sites—Baton Rouge, Alexandria, and Shreveport—available (they don't test in New Orleans, historically). But that is not always true. In 2022, if it returns to pre-pandemic form, there will be *four* total exams using a mix of sites and maximum registrants.

Going on past experience, you can predict that the June (or maybe July) exam and the December one will have no limits of candidates and will use the three

---

[3] There's a very good chance they will return to the 4x/year schedule like before the pandemic, if only to keep the numbers manageable for a particular administration. Spreading the tests out over a year prevents having to deal with enrollments beyond the physical limits of testing facilities and staff, and the hassle of spillover dates. For example, by having no summer 2021 exam as usual, the Sept. exam had more than 775 registrants a full three months before the exam date. And extensive spillover dates actually works out to their having to create more different exams than just four. But, by law, they are only *required* to give the exam "not less than twice per year."

cities as test sites. Candidates will be assigned to one of the available centers on the basis of their home address.

There should also be two more tests given, roughly in March and August. But those dates will be limited to the first 375 registrants—and administered only in Baton Rouge, at LSU's Himes Hall (probably in its large basement testing center). In many years past, it's a fact that the only spring and fall exams, if offered at all, were capped out at 375 and only at LSU. Early registration is essential for those test dates. Fortunately, you can see and count the list of registrants on the SOS site ("view scheduled applicants"), counting them to be sure it's not getting close to cut-off; beware, though, a surge of new registrants when test results are released from the previous administration, so you best apply before then—a month after the last test date. All of this will be updated on the website.

Admission letter and planning

Once you are registered for the notary exam, you'll receive notice to that effect (usually by email). Eventually you'll receive a letter (either mailed or attached to an email) that is essentially your ticket into the assigned test center for that test date only. Don't lose that ticket/letter or forget to bring it the day of the exam, along with proper identification.

Once you know for sure which test center and date is your exam, you can plan logistics for the day of the exam. You may be able to anticipate to near-certainty what test site will be yours if one of the three sites is obviously closer (e.g., New Orleans residents will get Baton Rouge), or there's only one site used for that test. Once you know or can guess with confidence, if you live far enough away (such as that New Orleans example), we strongly advise staying the night before nearby in a safe and quiet hotel. The test starts early in the morning, and late entrants may be barred from taking the exam and certainly will not get extended time. A flat tire or traffic issues could blow months of preparing for the exam. Plus having to get up very early to be sure to make the exam in time—and deal with parking issues at the test site—will leave you tired even before the exam starts. It's a grueling five-hour exam, so to maximize your focus and chances of passing, make it easy on yourself getting into the exam room rested and on time.

Americans with Disabilities Act accommodations

There's another layer of "registration" not discussed in depth here: the possibility of seeking accommodations under the Americans with Disabilities Act. This may include a quieter room than the massive Himes Hall basement which is the mainstay of their testing program (or what's typical at other sites). This effectively creates a whole other application process, for some candidates. The site, at https://www.sos.la.gov/NotaryAndCertifications/PrepareForTheNotaryExam/GetExamInformation/Pages/default.aspx, sets out the ADA process and rules. It is obvious that approval of accommodations takes time and is not granted as a matter of course. But the website suggests that requests with supporting documents submitted to LSU's testing office at least two weeks before the exam date will be evaluated and answered. So it's at least possible to apply for the exam at the last minute and then have a couple weeks to gather support for a request.

Some more exam-day issues related to the ADA are noted below in ch. 10.

7

FUNDAMENTALS STUDY GUIDE: INSERTS, TABS, AND NOTES

At this point you've "qualified" and ordered your *Fundamentals* study guide (ch. 4), taken the pre-assessment (ch. 5), and registered in time for the next administration of the exam (ch. 6). You should see your name and home parish (your domicile where you live and vote, not a work address) listed on the Secretary of State website on the page for "view scheduled applicants." Or, even before that point you bought the study guide, in anticipation of taking the exam.

The exam is open-book, allowing you to take *Fundamentals* in with you (and nothing else to look at, as we detail in ch. 10). But you can only use an edition of the same year the day of the exam. Buying an old, used edition ("old" meaning last year, even) is a waste of money unless you're just pre-studying for the next year anyway. Buying a new one this year when you plan to take the exam next year is a possible waste of money, too, unless getting a headstart on the substance of notary law is worth it to you.

In that case—if you're sure you are not taking the exam this year (e.g., you're already past the last time it's given) but you want to start studying for next— consider finding a cheap previous year's edition, even one several years old. It hasn't changed *that* much over the past several years, and you'll wind up buying and reading closely next year's new edition anyway, so there's not much premium on having the placeholder book, read only to get ahead, be brand new. Better yet, in the interim, borrow a library copy (even of one 2017 or later, I'd say) to get going, knowing that your more serious study (and writing into the book) will take place when you have a new one in hand. By the way, there's no eBook or PDF available of *any* year's edition.

The new edition is typically available on January 4 or so, though in some years printing delays have pushed it into much later in January—frustrating if you're trying to prepare for the first exam of the new year, and it's scheduled pretty early in March. (This is also very frustrating to us teachers of notary prep, since our students may not have the text until the class has already started.) Look for the new edition's release at the SOS page "Prepare for the Notary Exam" (it will suddenly show a different-color cover), or just join a Facebook group (ch. 11) where someone will announce the new edition is available. Even the study guide has its own Facebook page, and that too tells you it's now out, if you follow it.

Because you can only bring with you the current edition, it makes sense to take the exam in one of its first administrations of the year. That way if you do fail it, you have the right book to prepare and take the next time. Waiting until December to take the exam for the first time (or in 2021, the fall one is last) runs the risk that you'll have to buy a new book and write notes in it all over again for a March exam.

That's not the end of the world—it still may be worth the learning curve to go ahead take it late in one year even if you plan to study even harder for it in March with a new book—but it does extend your costs at least another $100. And a new edition of a book can be a bit disorienting if you've gotten used to certain subjects being in a specific location (like visually you've learned that the eight reasons to disinherit a kid are on the left side). Still, giving it a fair shot during the year's final administration is a good idea if the end result is you're more ready for another shot the next year, even with a new book and new notes.

No book or older book?

We haven't mentioned the possibility of studying an older edition then going into the actual exam with no book. It's allowed, but foolhardy. This is an open-book exam for a reason, and nearly impossible for anyone to pass without having the book the day of the exam. If you're doing that to save $100, consider that when you fail it, you'll pay $200 next time (plus processing fees), to finally get the book and to re-register for the next exam. The stories are legendary of people walking out of the exam early into it who either have no book with them or have one that looks like it's cracked open for the first time that day.

We also haven't mentioned sneaking in with the earlier edition, because they check, and forbid it. In fact, it's considered an act of cheating to bring with you any year's edition other than the one they specify for this administration. For 2021, their notice is: "Using any reference materials other than the 2021 edition of the study guide is considered an act of cheating and constitutes ground for dismissal from the text." (They mean *test*.) They say that's because notary law changes and the substantive information is outdated for "informed and accurate practice." But each new edition doesn't change *so* much that it'd be impossible to pass without reading the new book. (In fact in the first administration of 2021, due to the unusual cancellation of December's exam, they allowed either the new book or the previous year's—don't count on this happening again.)

The other reason seems to be to have a uniform set of materials all candidates have on test day, to make it easier and fairer to proctor. Or they want to sell more new books. Even if it makes sense to encourage the latest text, it's not clear why using an older one—even if foolish—would be "cheating."

No inserts in the book

Using the current *Fundamentals* book is an essential during the exam. It'd be great if you could also bring notes and study aids, too (such as an index from an outside source like ours). But you absolutely cannot. It has to be the whole book, intact and physically unaltered from any other pages. No loose sheets, inserts, post-its, or taped extra pages (or parts of pages) are permitted.

They could even consider it an act of cheating if you come in with any extra paper, attached or loose, though more likely they will just remove it (but don't tempt the proctors: they've told you they can dismiss you). You can't even take the errata sheet in with you—the sheet they added to the book after its release (they give it to you again, there).

The proctors actually spend a good time before the test begins screening each applicant not only for their admission letter and acceptable identification, but also to see that the book has no loose additions or attachments. They take your book and hold it by the spine to see if anything falls out or appears all extra. They may flip through it. The point is they check closely enough that you're not getting anything past them. You're stuck with the pages of the book you bought.

Limited tabbing is allowed

The one "attachment" you can add to your study guide is tabs, if you find them useful for locating specific subjects (more on that tactic below). But even then they are very specific about what tabs are allowed and at the very least will make you remove them—and potentially dismiss you, treating them as forbidden inserts—if yours don't conform. The only physical tab you can use is the "perma-nent" kind, which is hard to find at office stores and may have to be ordered from them online or Amazon. They say, "Tabs must be self-adhesive and must permanently attach to the edge of a page. Only one tab is allowed per page. Tabs must be no longer than two inches in length and must be of the clear plastic type." We find that Avery brand meets their specs, though if a certain variety comes out more than two inches in width, you should cut it to two. Note that Avery's "Ultra" tabs look cool but are repositional, so disallowed.

When they say "clear," they mean *transparent*. Color-coded but otherwise see-through plastic tabs are fine. In fact, that is the kind they show when you click on the link they provide as an example. Avery makes both clear-uncolored (item #16241 or 16221 at Amazon; 315473, 398453, or 314039 at Office Depot) and clear-colored (16219 or 16228 at Amazon; 933671 or 933689 at Office Depot) permanent tabs. The different item numbers are for various widths, from one inch to two. OfficeMax has its own item numbers but searching the above should take you to the right order page.

You are limited to one tab per page. They do not specify whether it must go along the sides or the top of the page. But not both, on one page.

You can write or print onto an insert that you slide into the sleeve of the fixed tab, such as "Requires Authentic Act" or "Wills & Successions." That's the point, of course. They are permanent in the sense of non-repositional, but if you do find you need to move them, you can certainly razor them out and place a new one elsewhere. If you just need to change the insert, there are extra blank white inserts in the pack with the tabs. More on tabbing in this chapter, to follow.

Writing into the book

They say "the pages may be marked up, highlighted or annotated." So, the book's a great place to take notes or transfer them from a class or study aid (see ch. 11). There's no cheating by writing into the book, or using a book that someone else has written into (if this year's). There's no rule on the number of colors of high-lighter you may use. You can write in the book as much as you want to, using pen or pencil, in whatever colors you wish. The words and annotations so inserted are not limited to your own original thoughts.

You can write on the blank inside-cover pages and other pages that have blank canvases, in whole or in part. The cover insides are especially good spots to add very important information that should be always handy, such as the skeleton of typical versions of authentic acts. You can create extra space to write on with white-out, as explained below.

In the process, turn the guide into what you want it to be, within the limits of these rules. It'll be more functional than in its original form. It makes little sense to take a lot of notes in a notebook or on a laptop, unless that's just a waypoint to adding the right ones—the best ones—somewhere into the guide itself. *You can't take the notebook in with you*, or print-outs from your typed notes. So we don't recommend you waste energy creating notes that can't be accessed—since you are perfectly permitted to take notes in the book itself up to its physical limits. I tell my students to take class notes as much as possible in the textbook itself.

Pens and pencils

While making notes in the book, I suggest using a fine-point mechanical pencil with hard lead and a good eraser. You'll probably have some false starts and misprints along the way that are best changed easily. Even ink is all right, but be prepared to resort to white-out when you realize you have better points to make than the ones you started with. Some of my students swear by erasable pens for this purpose—that makes sense, though I found a hard-leaded pencil worked fine on everything except places where white-out had been used.

Some specific pencil suggestions: a fine-point mechanical pencil (0.5mm, or certainly no more than 0.7, such as those from BIC) works well—though see ch. 10 for whether you can use it on the exam itself. Some pen suggestions: you may want to use a fine-point ballpoint pen (0.7mm, such as Zebra or Pilot). Don't use ink that smears or prevents you from writing as small as you can (and can read).

For any new surfaces you create with white-out, if you do, pencil works poorly and you may want to use ballpoint pen. Gel ink and other slick pens won't stick to this surface (and erasable pens may be problematic too).

White-out

Although there's no mention on the SOS website of using white-out (or Liquid Paper) in your book, it's a time-honored tradition taught by prep instructors throughout the state. It's obvious this is allowed, within the limits of not physically altering the book as such. It was an especially crucial art—literally—at a time that the study guide had few blank pages in it. Even with the new edition's blank 16 sides at the back, handy for notes or indexing the book, you may feel a need for more room to write notes and lists in the book beyond the blank pages at the end and blank spaces within the book.

Prep classes and workbooks have long advised creating new real estate inside the study guide in convenient places by using white-out over parts of the book that aren't useful on exam day (e.g., title page, copyright page, acknowledgments, endnotes of attribution, large quote blocks of legal history at the start of sections but repeated elsewhere). The proctors clearly allow you to use white-out judiciously so as not to alter it in any major way from the outside. They flip through it to determine whether you've attached notes. Mainly that's done by turning the book upside down, holding the spine. In the process you wouldn't want the white-out to come out so thick that it looks weird during their examination—like a page that doesn't sit right by its next page. The best way to do this is a few thin layers, with pausing and a little blowing perhaps, to allow drying between. Slathering it on won't work right.

Some students of mine report that they can do this best by using an actual paint brush to spread the Liquid Paper onto the surface. But my experience is that it works just fine either using the brush in the bottle or a white-out pen. You don't have to cover the old words so completely that no one can tell there was print underneath; you just have to be able to write over it, legibly.

On one Facebook group, some have reported that a superior method is to use white-out *tape*. I have no experience with the mechanics of this, but it's said to be easy and one-step compared to the more usual method of multiple passes and blowing. However, one member of the group reported that they saw someone get rejected at sign-in because the tape appeared too much like an attachment or insert into the book. I haven't verified this, but I'm skeptical it's an issue as long as the tape effectively creates a new surface on the page itself and is not just a paper on top of it that you write on. The effect of the tape *should* be just like brushing on Liquid Paper, and if that's so, it wouldn't be rejected by a proctor.

With the addition of blank pages to the 2021 *Fundamentals*, the main reason to use the white-out method of old is to have more notes near the actual location that's most relevant—if there are pages nearby that can be painted out with no loss of content (the material underneath is redundant or not particularly useful). Or to reserve those blank pages for class note-taking. In any event, it's up to you to turn the book into a full-service exam aid for test day, within their rules.

Are massive notes and tabbing worth the trouble?

Some candidates clearly overdo the addition of material and the whiting out of pages to make room for even more notes. On the day of the exam, you probably won't consult most of the textual notes (better use can be made of *indexing*, cross-referencing, lists, and charts). It's not about having the most information; it's about finding the right information the day of the exam, though of course the process of writing the notes is itself educational.

Similarly, although tabbing is allowed, many people on the Facebook groups report that their tabs got in the way of flipping through pages fast more than they guided them to the right page. They used too many tabs and wished they hadn't. What they thought they would need an entrée to (e.g., a list of acts that must be authentic, currently pp. 301-303), turned out to have a location so well-known after intensive studying that they could turn to that page easily. And the examiners have a habit of testing on things found in multiple places in the book, or in the "wrong" place in it, such that the tabbing was at best one possible location (so indexing became a better way). Tabs just don't work out to be much help.

Even so, if this is a way you typically prepare a book for an exam, or organize documents at your work, there's little risk to your adding tabs. Perhaps you should make notes to yourself along the way where tabs *might* go but wait until late in the process to finalize those. In my own experience, I started with ten or so tabs I *thought* would be helpful, but eventually wound up cutting most out, leaving only a few for the most crucial transitions in the book (e.g., that list of acts now on p. 301; the glossary section, where I'd inserted an index by hand). I didn't touch even these tabs, as it turned out. By then I knew where the broad strokes were, and I used indexing and cross-references to find specifics.

A *different way of tabbing*

Two members of a Facebook study group have used an artistic and innovative replacement for tabbing. And I saw similar examples with test-takers on exam day. They use various color highlighters to paint the outer (side) edge of the pages of a chapter, changing colors at a new chapter. They then wrote the chapter topic or some short signifier on the outside page edges as well. Thus, ch. 24 on testaments and successions could all be lime green on the outside (viewing the book from the side), turning light red at the ch. 25 on trusts. On the side in block letters would be written WILLS in the green area and TRUSTS in the red ones.

This way avoids attaching any plastic which can slow down flipping through pages, but still gives you a visual place to quickly move to a subject-location in the book. If you use this method, consider grouping some of the shorter chapters together as one "part" and one color, such as ch. 1-6 on Louisiana and civil law.

As suggested above for tabs, we doubt such artistry is necessary: you will know where the wills chapter is from reading it a few times and flipping to it taking practice exams. Or even all that helpful: a question nominally on "testaments" may be answered not by looking in ch. 24 on wills but in ch. 27 on small successions, ch. 8 on community property, or ch. 19 on appearance clauses. That's one of the reasons the exam is so hard. Just knowing a general place in the book for a topic is not likely to lead to easily answering all questions related to the subject. Still, the color-edge way offers a convenient crutch on exam day without having plastic get in the way, and may also be useful during studying to visualize where the main topics are.

8

Format of the Exam and Questions

The notary exam, as reimagined starting just the past few years by the Secretary of State's office and LSU's testing center, is all multiple choice. It involves no written component any more, as it did five or six years ago. It's a five-hour exam. Its usual format is 72 to 80 questions (often about 75). Almost always, there are four options to choose from—with a smattering of questions offering five choices, but never just two or only true-false as such.

To be sure, some questions will be worded in terms of true-false options, but still leaving four or five choices for you to pick from. For example, after a statement of facts or reference to a scenario (fact pattern), the call of the question may be something like: "Which one of the following [four or five] statements is false?" One format they've occasionally used makes choice D or E as "None of the above" or "All of the above." Fortunately this doesn't seem to be used a lot on any particular exam.

There's no penalty for guessing wrong—no deduction, no counting-off—so you should fill in one dot for every question asked, leaving no empty answers. A student reported that the person next to her was leaving three or four blank even with minutes to go to fill them in. That makes no sense. Every possible point matters.

Only one answer is correct or "best." Don't fill in more than one dot per question, or the machine will count it as wrong. If you filled in an answer and change your mind, erase your first choice thoroughly. Usually on multiple choice exams, the standard advice is not to change your mind too often. You should probably second-guess your first instinct only if you have a concrete reason to change the answer or you find the source of your error in the *Fundam*entals guide itself. Otherwise you may as well leave your first choice alone.

There are two versions of the exam in the testing room on exam day: "A" and "B." They are actually the same exam overall but with the questions rearranged (and particular answer-choices moved, too) so as to discourage copying from a neighbor. The arrangement is not supposed to make a difference in terms of difficulty or making sense of the questions; it just changes the answer key used.

Scenarios

Many of the specific questions follow after a hypothetical fact pattern they call a "scenario." This is a relatively short story (usually 5 to 10 lines or less) of people trying to accomplish something or presenting a notary problem, setting up a question or series of questions. The series often make the next question change something in the facts, and asks a different question, making it a moving target.

For example, the original scenario may be stated in terms of a donation of a plot of land by Jane and Mark, a husband and wife, to John. But a question or two later they will ask you to assume that it is now a watch; or that Jane is donating it without Mark knowing it; or that it's a sale not a donation. You have to adapt on the fly and not get lost in the facts. In the above examples, you'd need to recognize that the donation rules are quite different for land versus watches; that donation by one part of a married couple can be problematic, depending on community property rules (or at least changes the appearance clause of an act); and that the way notaries execute sales is different from how donations are done.

As these examples illustrate, the "scenario" approach makes you work from a fact pattern that names people who have specific roles in a transaction or situation, making you keep them straight. It also makes you *apply* the notary law you've learned (or can find in the book during the exam) to a set of facts, not just answering a question in the abstract.

Library documents

Related to this approach is the use of "library documents." They will give you, in addition to a question book and a scantron sheet (and probably the errata sheet for the study guide), a separate packet of documents to which you refer when asked in specific questions. This library is usually some kind of notarial act or legal instrument such as a will, power of attorney, or mortgage. It's probably flawed in several ways, incomplete, or marked with specific clauses (such as "line A") that can be referenced in a question. The question will itself be based on a larger scenario, and inside of that will be the direction to consider and answer questions from the named library document. In any exam of some 75 questions, they are likely to give you two or three library documents. An example would be to tether 30 of the 75 questions, more or less, to two different library documents.

Is the whole exam based on scenarios and library documents?

The Secretary of State's website pretty much states that *all* questions relate to some scenario that in turn references a library document they provide: "Applicants will read scenarios that are typical of notarial practice in Louisiana. Each scenario is accompanied by a library of documents referenced in the scenario. Applicants respond to multiple-choice items drawn from the content of the scenarios...." This is a bit misleading, though these formats are used enough in the exam that it's understandable that they'd emphasize it.

In reality, it's very unlikely that every scenario links to a library document (*most* scenarios will likely be independent of any external document beyond the scenario set-up). And it is likely they'll give you several stand-alone questions unconnected to any scenario. They really can, and do, frame questions in the abstract, asking for instance "what is the notary's 'seal'?" without making it part of a fact pattern (answer: their signature). They can ask "which of the following rules about donations is true?" and not link it to a scenario. The website simply ignores this framing of the question, though probably *most* of your questions relate at least loosely to a scenario. I say "loosely" because sometimes it will be a very tenuous jumping-off point to asking a question that is, really, about as straightforward and abstract as the "seal" one, but *technically* is a scenario, e.g., "In a sale of a condo from Paul to Grace, the notary's 'seal' is: ...." Yes, that's a "scenario," but really the question is readily understood to ask for a broader rule that applies far beyond these facts.

At any rate, the assumption that *all* questions follow from scenarios is exaggerated. But you may as well study as if they are, because that makes the questions a little bit harder than if they were asked in a direct way.

Questions answered from several pages in the study guide

As noted above, some questions are worded in a globally positive or negative way, such as: "Which of the following statements is false?" This format often tests your ability to know (or find) choices from several places in the book, because the options don't have to be related in subject matter to each other. And similarly when the set-up asks, "Which of the following is true?"

Even outside the true-false format with four options, many questions force you to use two or more different places in the book to answer the question as a whole. They can do this by breaking down the information in the book over two places; an example is the law of mortgages, split between ch 18 and 21 in the study guide. Or the question itself makes you relate together two different rules to merge into one answer. An example (that you need not understand yet) is: this small succession is an affidavit (ch. 27 in the guide); affidavits can't be done via power of attorney (ch. 20—not in the chapters on affidavits or powers of attorney!); therefore, answer C is wrong because it's having an agent sign for one of the heirs on the succession form.

So, you should study and mark up the book in such a way that you can quickly go to multiple pages, to read the right answer or to merge two ideas into one right answer. This puts a premium on indexing and cross-referencing, as found in our resources cited in ch. 11.

Distractors and "best" answer

At the top of the exam question booklet, the examiners emphasize that it's a search for the "best" answer, among the choices presented. They may consciously include a "distractor" that is OK as far as it goes, or partly right, but doesn't fully resolve the essential issue in the question—and doesn't count. It may be right for a narrow reason when the larger concern you can see they are trying to test by the question as a whole is not met. So, the distractor is one that is true in some technical or limited way, when another answer is more consistently or unconditionally correct.

To be sure, there are plenty of questions with only one right answer, and this dilemma of the tempting distractor at worst narrows you down to two decent options. So it shouldn't intimidate you too much. Just be aware of how they do that at times and the need to read all choices.

On the Facebook groups, those who just took their exam and offer a post-mortem often say that the hardest thing about the exam is choosing the "best" answer when they think two are correct. Their concern is understandable, and you have to prepare for the exam keeping in mind this possibility.

However, I actually believe (and observed in taking the test) that almost all of the questions they ask and count do reduce to one correct answer (and certainly do this more than it *feels* to a test-taker, at the time). Another answer may look OK but doesn't really apply to the scenario facts, so it's not really right even if it is a true statement in the abstract. Or an answer that appears right is actually incorrect for some picky or technical reason that would be found in the study guide if the test-taker had more time. In any event, our workbook of sample questions and answers discussed in ch. 11 illustrates many ways in which one answer is truly "best" in the face of a distractor.

9

PASSING SCORE

Your goal should be to get 75% correct of the questions that count. By "questions that count," I mean that you can assume that some of the 75 or so questions they ask are experimental or controls in some way. They may be testing its viability for using as a question-that-counts on a future exam. You can't know which, of course, so you have to treat all questions the same, even if they feel unexpected. For purposes of keeping the numbers discussed below simple, let's pretend that there are 75 questions and all of them matter. Even if that's not so in absolute numbers, the ratios below still hold.

So, the *official* goal is 75%. That's because the SOS notary division assures you: "To pass the examination, the applicant must correctly answer at least 75% of the items." But really getting 70% right almost always passes, too. They promise you'll pass at 75, but historically they accept a lower score even if you cannot count on it. They suggest this by adding: "Post-test statistical analysis of exam items, however, may provide a basis for adjusting the passing score." That suggests that some specific questions may not count for anyone after this analysis, but the crucial impact of the post-test adjustment has usually been in lowering the passing score for everyone to about a 70.

Letting you know the results

You won't know the actual target, though, until you get your score in an email from LSU and a curt statement of "passing" or "not passing." They don't allow re-examination of your exam or score, and they don't tell you what you missed or why. You won't learn from all your mistakes because no one will tell you what's mistaken. It's just not a very transparent process. This is true even though the site promises, "La. R.S. 35:191.1 (A)(3) makes a provision for review of examinations." Apparently they mean their own post-test analysis, done without you.

The much-anticipated email often comes about a month after your exam date (though lately that's varied from two to six weeks, likely with all the spillover dates compressing LSU's work). Facebook group members—dying to hear—regularly moan, understandably, that it shouldn't take a month to run exams through a scantron-reader. But invariably someone replies that if it takes them more time to do the post-test adjustment, to the benefit of candidates, then please take your time. I honestly have no idea what their grading and post-exam reconsideration process is like and why it takes a month; I do think it tends to benefit test-takers, at least in making the 75% target not fixed in stone.

The email usually is sent out in a blast to candidates around 4:00 to 4:30 in the afternoon. The email goes to the one you used when qualifying (another reason you can't do the whole process with forms and faxes). Keep an eye on your spam folder. Mass emails to, say, 750 applicants tempts most email systems to assume it's an attempt to get you to buy Viagra or date seniors in your neighborhood.

The numbers you need aren't so daunting

As challenging as many questions on the exam will seem, or the exam as a whole even, keep in mind that there's a decent margin of error to earn a passing score. Since 70% usually passes, and they'll have as many as 80 questions, you can miss around 24 questions and still pass. Knowing this should ease the pressure some, especially for any one question that risks bogging you down (say, a tough property description one). I recognize that not all of the 80 questions are scored, as some are experimental, but the logic of this *ratio* still applies: if all 80 counted, you'd need to get 56 right, and so on for smaller numbers.

This also means that in a section of 15 questions, and assuming five such groups (a total of 75 questions), you can miss *four* questions in each group and still leave room to miss a couple more here or there, and yet pass. You can set a realistic goal for any one question, or any one section, and not be overly intimidated.

Knowing that there is a healthy margin of error should boost your confidence, both in preparing for the exam, and during the test day itself as you go.

In addition, the pass rate discussed in ch. 1 should be less daunting than it first appears. Yes, it's a challenging exam, and that pass rate is lower than a typical professional licensure exam, such as the bar exam. So, prepare seriously. But don't get overwhelmed or psyched out by the bare math of past pass rates. Consider that many test-takers have observed other candidates leaving early or looking lost because they were not prepared. Some had no study guide with them, and many had one that looked like this was its first day of use. The exam is open to many people who are not prepared or motivated to take it seriously, and it shows. There is no screening process before the exam (unlike with, say, a bar exam), such that all results come down to this one performance. The only pre-assessment does no screening other than encouraging self-reflection of aptitude and interest; and yet the exam is taken by many people who do not take advantage of that (not so much this one score, as we point out in ch. 5, but the overall self-assessment one should do before embarking on this journey).

At any rate, the pass rate for this exam does not capture the victory available to those who take it seriously, start preparing early, learn the concepts of the study guide, and are able to find specifics the day of the exam. If you are doing those things, that reality supports confidence as well.

10

DAY OF THE EXAM

Here are some important rules and facts about the day of the exam:

- It is a five-hour exam. Although in a different context the Secretary of State website refers to "the break," there really isn't one. It's a continuous five hours without a break. Any bathroom breaks happen because you raise your hand and a proctor accompanies you to the (outside area of the) bathroom, and hopefully a water fountain there. It's grueling.

- The only book you can have with you is the current edition of the *Fundamentals* study guide. The rules allowing marking it up, and prohibiting inserts and attachments, are discussed in our ch. 7.

- No other materials or resources are allowed, except what they hand you after check-in. *No notebooks or outlines.*

- No smart watch may be worn, even if turned off. *No Apple watch.*

- If your phone or other electronic device you may have with you makes a sound, they will dismiss you from the exam. This includes subtle buzzing and vibrating. *Just leave it in the car.* Don't risk dismissal because a device you think is off actually is on, or even *is* off but goes through some kind of update that makes it reboot (this has happened in my law classes). If you're dismissed, you fail—no refunds. *Leave Fitbit outside, too.*

- This rule against devices making sounds includes watches, which even if not "smart" may well have an alarm feature you don't realize is set to sound during the five hours. Leave it in the car, unless it's so old in its design that it can't possibly make a sound (my cheap analog Timex).

- You don't really need a watch anyway. The test centers have large wall clocks visible from all seats. But just in case, you may want to borrow an analog watch from someone—a watch that has *no* electronic features or sound. Once you confirm that your vantage point allows you to see their clock, put even the old, silent watch away in a purse or pocket so that if somehow it buzzes (you were wrong about its alarm function), it won't be heard. Still, the foolproof way is to leave it outside. Even if you can't see the clocks, they announce times verbally along the way.

- "Timers" are prohibited. Presumably they allow dumb watches, but don't test the proctors by bringing a clock or countdown item. *No wicked-witch hourglasses.*

- You are not allowed to access your cellphone even if you have finished your own exam, while you're still in the testing room. *No Instagram.*

- The SOS site says, "Eating, drinking, and the use of tobacco or reading materials are not permitted in the testing room." It does you no good to bring a water bottle. At least at the LSU test site, they have a water fountain near the bathrooms; plus drink and snack machines you can access *before* check-in. I suspect they have similar facilities at the other sites. *No Propel or other bourgy hydration.*

- The site also warns, "Any applicant exhibiting disruptive behavior may be dismissed." *No rioting.* But seriously, don't distract your neighbors.

- ADA accommodations of any kind must be applied for at least two weeks in advance. They won't accommodate you on the fly, no matter what documentation you bring with you. If you're accommodated, you know that ahead of time. See our ch. 6.

- The website isn't clear about this, but they prohibit you from writing *into* the *Fundamentals* book during the exam (presumably to prevent people from copying the questions to teach others about the exam). If you're not careful, you'll find yourself circling some part of it you want to come back to, or making a note in the margin that applies to another question you read. Instead, mark such reminders on the other materials they give you, such as the question booklet or the library-document handout.

- If you finish early enough—fifteen minutes or more before the five hours are up—you may quietly gather your things, check out, and leave the room. Once it's fifteen minutes from the end, you have to wait in your seat quietly until time is called for everyone and the general check-out process begin. Follow all instructions at check-out exactly.

- Writing after time is called, even filling in a couple of dots mindlessly, is grounds for dismissal and failure. People report that they've seen this happen!

In addition their formal rules, here are some reminders and process information you may want to know about the day of the exam.

Pencils

Have plenty of sharpened #2 pencils on hand, perfect for scantrons. Some Facebook group members say they took, and used, a pencil sharpener during the exam. I suppose this can be done as long as its noise doesn't violate the rule against distracting others. It just seems easier to me to bring extra pencils. I also suspect that if you raised your hand to call a proctor over (as you do when you need a bathroom sortie), they could score you a pencil.

Not found on the list above, because it's probably not an official policy and not mentioned on their website, is the question whether you can use a mechanical pencil on the exam. I did, and thought nothing of it. But a Facebook member posted he'd heard it's not allowed. When I called the notary division, after some asking around, they said not to use one. So, I guess it's disallowed, if not likely to get you dismissed from the exam. I suspect their statement to me is not about a "rule" but because they want to be sure all pencils are #2 lead; perhaps some mechanical leads won't work well for scantron readers. If you take mechanical pencils, be sure they have #2 lead. In fact, I still advise having one mechanical pencil with you just in case your regular ones break.

Check-in

The Secretary of State website discusses rules and policies for taking the exam, but it doesn't give a flavor of how involved the check-in process is. Be ready for it taking an hour or more just to get to the point of starting the exam. Even the line to get into an exam room starts to queue well before the check-in time they tell you. Give yourself plenty of time to find parking (another reason to spend the night before nearby rather than trying to drive an hour or more to get there). First organizing the queue by alphabet and entryways, it takes time even to get to the screening part at the test-room door.

Before the set time, eat enough, but not too much, to last until well after noon. There may be snack machines nearby you can use while queuing before check-in starts, and it's best to use those while you can. Better yet, you can bring food and drink *to* the site as long as you don't bring it into the exam room. If going without food for possibly six hours (adding in the potential check-in time) is medically risky for you, consider seeking accommodations under the ADA (see our ch. 6) not for a special test room but simply to be allowed a snack bar or special drink. Without approval of that access ahead of time, you can't eat or drink during the exam.

Because there's no drinking, unless they provide a water fountain at any bathroom breaks you may take, you may have some difficulty taking medicines along the way. Be sure to disclose your need to do so to the proctors during sign-in, so it doesn't appear during the exam that you are eating—and to be able to have access to water to take the medicine. I was able to take some meds I need regularly by full disclosure in check-in, and the proctors were understanding.

At check-in at the door, they require identification and the admission letter they sent or emailed to you a week or so before the exam. People do forget to bring the letter for some reason. So, as soon as you receive it, make a copy to put in your car trunk, wallet, or purse—something you will have for sure on exam day. Also, take a picture on your phone. If all else fails, the examiners may accept an image of it. Then turn your phone off and, if possible, put it back in your car.

If your admission letter or email tells you to bring a mask, make sure you do. Indeed, it's best to have one with you regardless of whether they'll make you wear it. If it turns out they require one, you won't be left scrambling for someone to lend an extra.

The next step is when they screen everyone for acceptable appearance of their *Fundamentals* book. This takes time, too, because it's a careful physical process.

Then they give assign you to a seat, and even then take a lot of time before they hand out test materials and actually start the test. For example, they first have you fill out a survey that establishes you meet the qualifications and provides other data points that they presumably use to answer educational research questions later about who passes and who doesn't.

They also take time before starting the exam to go over rules and policies (some of the bulletpoints above). They explain the process for seeking a bathroom trip.

Time per question

You should go into the exam aware of how long you'll spend on any one question. Commit to spending no more than three or four minutes even on the hardest question, mark your best guess, move on, and come back to that one if you have time. 300 minutes divided by 75 questions is 4.00. Some easier questions take far less and buy time (they do have a few low-hanging fruit on every exam, testing basic rules you'll know by heart at that point). But you also may need time for a bathroom break or two and a water-fountain sortie.

Taking practice exams not only helps you learn notary law and exam format, it also helps you develop a rhythm and an instinct about when it's time to move on to the next question. And knowing that you really have less than five minutes per question, and that many questions are answered from multiple places in the study guide, supports the preparation strategy of writing an index and specific cross-references into your book.

Challenge to questions?

One of the materials they may give you is a "challenge" sheet. They say, "All items presented on the test are subjected to post-test statistical analysis that may provide a basis for adjustments to the passing score. Additionally, at the test administration, applicants may request a form on which they may challenge the validity of any item as written." More likely they will give everyone such a form, and you're allowed to fill it in during the exam. Probably it's a waste of time unless you find yourself at the end with extra time.

In my view the only reason you'd take advantage of this opportunity is if you think a question or two is ambiguous in such a way that you can explain *why* you picked the answer you do. There's a chance they would count a "wrong" answer as correct if your challenge to it explains away the perceived ambiguity well enough that it shows you got what they were going for, and know the law. But it's certainly a waste of time to use this form to vent generally about the way they frame many questions or ask for the "best" among answers you think are correct. They aren't going to change their reason for existence based on your complaint.

End of exam

Even this process takes a little bit of time when you'd rather be out getting a drink and sharing stories with fellow test-takers. Once time is called, stop writing immediately and sit there until your packet of materials is checked and all loose papers are collected. Do not write anything, or fill in any pencil dots on the answer sheet.

To avoid being tragically dismissed at this late stage by writing past the end of times, keep an eye on the test center's clocks. Spend the last four or five minutes making sure you've answered every question asked. There's no penalty for a wrong answer, so there's absolutely no reason not to guess on the last few questions—or even fill in dots without looking at the question if you must—to make sure all questions get counted.

Did you pass? You probably won't know for a few weeks, at best. See our ch. 9. It's also commonly stated in the Facebook groups that a call to the SOS notary division after a few weeks doesn't get you much useful or accurate information as to when you'll find out.

11

AVAILABLE BOOKS, CLASSES, AND OTHER RESOURCES

Knowing the format, rules, and process for the exam itself gives you an understanding of how (and how hard) you need to prepare to pass it. So, long before you take it, you have some decisions to make. Here is our summary of some of the study resources, including books, classes, and shorter coursework, that you should consider.

Classes

There is no formal educational criterion to taking the notary exam (except a high school diploma). No notary class is required. Plenty of candidates over the years have passed it without taking a formal class, perhaps simply by studying *Fundamentals* intensely. But I suspect that even the class-less who succeed use other resources such as workbooks and supplemental readings, and don't do it totally "alone." At any rate, unless it is impractical by schedule or clearly unaffordable, of course a class is recommended.

The exam's just hard enough—and the readings so complex and dense—that it makes sense to take an organized course of study. We do discuss guides and resources besides classwork below, and they're certainly recommended too, but any introductory book worth your money wouldn't lie to you and say it's easy to pass the exam without taking a class. It's not even easy to pass it *with* one. Let's just say that classes likely increase the odds of passing.

Full-length, in-depth classes tend to run from about 35 to 45 total hours of classroom component (plus they require, of course, a lot of outside reading and, hopefully, exercises and practice exams). That works out in many cases to about a 12-week series of once-a-week night classes of three hours each. Some are done online and remotely, but most of them meet in person (at least they did before the pandemic and probably will return to that structure). They tend to cost between $550 and $650.

There are many well-regarded notary prep classes, and by rule they must be taught by a notary with state-wide jurisdiction (which means they're either lawyers or have passed the state-wide, standardized notary exam given after 2005). The SOS notary office doesn't particularly recommend any, of course, but they do require them to register and, for private offerings, post a completion bond. The latter prevents an instructor from signing students up but failing to offer the class, at least without recourse to the students.

This book is not in a position to recommend against any particular teacher or course, either. I can say that I've heard good things—or read them in our Facebook groups—about several instructors and their dedication (not to the detriment of those I just don't know). Most notably these include Wendy Hilker at Loyola, Jennifer Brown at LSU-Shreveport, Lisa McCoy in Denham Springs, Carolyn Estilette in Jennings, Nan Riffe in Gonzalez, and Kara Williams at Delgado. Plus:

The most popular remote-online class is by Shane Milazzo (offered through his website or various university extension programs). His site has many ecstatic testimonials. He is knowledgeable and affable, and the online format is convenient and allows playback of the classes you took (or missed), up until the exam.

Donaldson Educational Systems out of Metairie, using experienced instructors, is popular and eventually should return to a combined in-class format using simultaneous state-of-the-art remote access. It's part of a successful school with many career offerings, including business and real estate training.

Most notary prep classes don't offer college credit (nor should they, if they serve your purpose of passing the exam). Even those affiliated with universities and community colleges are usually considered "extension" or "continuing education" (non-credit) classes. But I am pretty sure that Fred Davis's very successful class at ULL gives accredited college credit (with ULL tuition). I am confident that Davis's in-class course, for those who take it seriously and complete the assignments, produces a high pass rate. His website's many testimonials, too, are very supportive.

My own academic Louisiana Notary Law class is at Tulane's School of Professional Advancement. It's available for non-Tulane students who sign up at SoPA, but most of the students are Tulane undergraduate or paralegal certificate students; that's because it costs more than traditional notary prep classes, due to its college credit. As much as I enjoy it, I don't recommend it for non-Tulane students unless you also want it to offer such credit for transfer to your program. So, ironically, I don't really push it here. Having said that, I welcome interested students to contact SoPA. It's remotely taught summer 2021, but probably will return to live in-class format spring 2022, in Elmwood.

Other than those, as far as I know, all notary classes are without credit and accreditation, but provide information to the Secretary of State. See the list of about 30 possible classes, information, registration, and contact information at https://www.sos.la.gov/NotaryAndCertifications/NotaryEducationProviderInformation/Pages/default.aspx.

It's tricky to do more than list the classes out there, but I am confident that what I say is supported—if incomplete from my lack of familiarity with other classes. I'm also confident that any of the classes serves its purposes and should be recommended over no class. We welcome thoughts and reviews shared on the two Facebook groups mentioned below. Talk amongst yourselves and develop better consumer data than my ideas and the SOS list of registered providers.

Ultimately, it requires honest self-evaluation to determine whether you can forego a full-length class and still give yourself a fair chance to pass. And you're probably in the best position to know whether your best style of learning—in-person by classroom vs. remotely, online—is physically available to you from the SOS list.

Shorter courses

Fred Davis regularly holds a popular seminar and workshop, in-person in a Lafayette hotel, about five weeks before most exams. It's listed as a product on his site www.passmynotary.com. He sums up some very testable subjects, explains the format of the questions, answers questions, and workshops practice questions—all on a Saturday morning. This year he's expanding it to a full day. It's cheaper if combined with his workbooks, below. He makes clear it's not a crash course, but tees up the exam in detail. It's been offered successfully for years.

Shane Milazzo records with students, for video access to customers, about eight hours of summaries of several important areas of notary law, such as wills and successions; property transfers and mortgages; and property descriptions. It's the "iPrep" on-demand offering on his site www.iNotaryNow.com, and it includes an original notebook of sample acts and some test questions.

On my site www.notarysidepiece.com, candidates can register for two interactive Zoom seminars (or view their recordings). One is an inexpensive "big picture" intro of notary law and the exam, for 3.5 hours on a Saturday. It's past the level of registration process but presents a preview with PowerPoints of the substance of notary rules and the exam for those who are fairly early on in their studying. The other is a "final lap" review seminar on Zoom for 5.5 hours a month before the test date, going over the most testable subjects and working in detail through a sample exam provided before the class. (In addition, my wife Michele and I teach a how-to-practice class for those who pass.) These sessions don't assume or require that participants buy my books.

Lisa McCoy, of www.realmotionnotaryservices.com, sometimes offers in-person sessions (in Denham Springs) on specific subjects, in addition to her prep lecture series. For example, on July 10, 2021, she focused on mandates and procurations. There may be other short-course offerings out there as well.

Facebook study groups

Currently there are two groups you can join on Facebook that support preparing for the exam, each having more than 650 members—both candidates and those who passed but stuck around to help. One is "Louisiana Notary Study Group," administered primarily by Denise Turbinton (always ready with a statutory cite to support her points). The other is "Louisiana Notary Exam Study Group," administered by founder David Ambrogio and myself (who fell into it, as a fan). Most members join both. Ask questions, post problems, practice scenarios, form study groups, and vent about the process.

In-person study groups

Traditionally, many people have formed private study groups as an inexpensive alternative to classes (or to meet outside of class and study together). That's been harder during the pandemic—or maybe easier since everyone got good at Zoom. They promote mutual support and reinforce staying on schedule. Participants can explain hard concepts to each other. It all comes down to whether you learn best and more efficiently alone vs. the peer pressure and focus of friends going through the same process as you.

Probably the best places to form such groups is online by asking at the Facebook groups, or around class times by asking classmates. My own opinion—admittedly biased because I am a provider and teach for a living—is that study groups are not a real substitute for a class.

Books

Many of the classes above use workbooks or study aids as part of their syllabus. They may be produced by the instructor (e.g., Milazzo or McCoy), or they may assign some of the ones below. At the very least, the most effective classes will explain the study guide, assign exercises, and give practice exams.

Independent of classes, serious self-study requires more help than *Fundamentals* provides. It's not considered the most organized and crystal-clear textbook. Almost all candidates, whether in class or studying at home, wind up using some of these extra resources. Here are the leading books not written for a specific class, but often used in them, or as part of serious self-study.

Davis

Fred Davis has two workbooks that are very detailed, helpful, and popular. The first, "critical knowledge," has hundreds of sample questions, with answers, based on scenarios and library documents. It also has many pages summarizing the most important areas of notary law in clear bulletpoints, and a sample structure of authentic acts. Many people have used this book over the years as a self-study course, and swear by it. The second, "general knowledge," is mainly sample exams of notary practice (covering, among other topics, the first seven chapters of *Fundamentals*, but less based on scenarios than the critical one). It relates to a time when the exam had a closed-book component of notary history and practice, but since those topics still come up on the exam (now open-book), this book remains useful. Both are available on his website and shipped quickly.

Childress

My two books, besides this one, are inexpensively found on Amazon, B&N, and other online stores (and in eBook at such sites as Kindle and Apple). They're meant to be a clutch part of serious self-study or add to classroom study. The first, *Louisiana Notary Exam Sidepiece to the 2021 Study Guide*, has tips, study tactics, exam strategies, extensive paginated cross-references, and examples of testable acts—advice far beyond this book. It explains community property in successions. Importantly, it adds a detailed index that *Fundamentals* (inexplicably) completely lacks, helpful when studying and to write into the guide to use the day of the exam. Many people have commented that the exam is unmanageable without such a complete index, especially since questions may cover different parts of the text. The second, *Louisiana Notary Exam Sample Questions and Answers 2021*, has 130 examples with right and wrong answers explained in detail, referencing pages in the guide. The explanations offer tactics and decode the "trick" of the way they sometimes frame questions or how they view one correct answer as "better" than another.

On the Facebook groups, many people comment that their best course of study was not an either/or, as they found value in using competitor study books. They don't see them as mutually exclusive. Participants offer their honest views of the advantages of each resource out there, so that's another reason to join a group.

"Educational Testing Group" as Author

A book that *sounds* like it would be great, and is cheap on Amazon, is something we can't endorse in good conscience. It's called *Louisiana Notary Public Exam*. Yet its own description says "it does not include any study guide." More importantly, its sample questions don't relate to Louisiana notary law or the tested *Fundamentals* substance in any meaningful way. You'd learn some national notary rules that Louisiana doesn't apply or test. At best it would distract you from learning things that *could* be tested; at worst it teaches you wrong. An example that shows its title is misleading: a question in its Test 2 that begins, "A county clerk is an elected county official..." Really? In what "county"? San Diego?

Other Books

However, a really good book to consider *after* passing the exam—but covers so much practice not tested in our state, though still relevant and useful—is the National Notary Association's *Notary Home Study Course*. It sounds like this would be sample questions for some other state's exam, but it's more like a comprehensive textbook of the day-to-day life of most notaries. So, it's not that nationally focused books have no place in your notary library. It's just that they don't help on *this* exam, your priority. Even if they stick "Louisiana" in the title.

Likewise, a great book to add to your library in the long run will be the Louisiana Notary Association's latest *Notary Survival Kit*, edited by Lisa McCoy. It has many forms for acts, suggested stamps and fee rates, and other information for new notaries. It's not so much a study aid for the notary exam, but it's useful for practicing notaries, as is membership in the LNA and/or another organization, Professional Civil Law Notaries Association. Both provide continuing education for notary practitioners.

You'll eventually want on your bookshelf a copy of the latest edition of the Louisiana Civil Code. A two-volume paperback version by West Publishing Co. is sold at a discount for members of the LNA.

Finally, the publisher of this book and the *Sidepiece* offers a book by Greg Rome and Stephan Kinsella, *Louisiana Civil Law Dictionary*. It explains terminology and legal concepts in more detail than the study guide's glossary, and covers more Louisiana law. In paperback or eBook formats, it's inexpensive for all that it provides.

Other study resources

The internet sells flash cards of Louisiana notary law terms and phrases. These could be quite useful if you learn best with flash cards, as many do. But really they are just sheets of definitions straight out of the study guide's glossary, so they don't add much to your existing book. Because the sheets have to be cut up anyway, it's fair to say that it's almost as easy for you to create your own flash cards by photocopying pages in the glossary, cutting the definition, and writing the term on the back.

Some members of the Facebook study groups say great things about Quizlet. It's free and also in the form of digital flash cards to memorize Louisiana notary terms. One such slide show is found at https://quizlet.com/16576817/flashcards.

Twelve free practice questions are available on Davis's PassMyNotary website under the heading "Sample Questions." The *Fundamentals* book also has some sample questions and answers in the back. You probably shouldn't look at these until you've read enough of the study guide that they are realistic practice for you.

Finally, friends of yours who are lawyers or practicing notaries can answer questions for you and certainly explain big-picture concepts. But keep in mind—as I warn my students in Louisiana Notary Law but also in my Evidence class—that there is the practical answer and then there's the (bar) exam answer. For you, this means you need to focus first and foremost on the right answer as stated in *Fundamentals* and tested by the state. It's not always the same as what you'd be told by others.

12

SOME INTRODUCTORY LAW ENGLISH[4]

Although our Introduction promised that this is not the book to explain notary law in general or the *Fundamentals* study guide, those who are just beginning to read it ought to know at the outset some terms and phrases that come up in the book and may be confusing. Its Glossary defines most of the relevant substantive law terms, and there are other sources available to learn Louisiana law terms in more detail.[5] None of that is attempted here, of course.

Nevertheless, my students tell me that there are some legal terms or other wordings used in the *Fundamentals* book that tend to slow them down. A little decoding may be helpful. I don't mean notary law terms. I mean other words that people in law use all the time that got stuck into the study guide as if the whole world already knows them. When you see these in the book, or in notary practice, here's the code:

- *supra* means *above*—and *infra* means *below*, like later in a case opinion. It makes no sense that the law would use Latin terms of the same syllables and letter count as "above" and "below," but there you are.

- *Id.* is a signal that repeats a citation (from a case or statute) that was just cited. Just look to the last citation (often a line or two up from the *Id.*) and read this as "the same citation you just said." In English lit, it's *Ibid.*

- *ff.* means *following*, like the next pages. So, referring you to pages 168ff. means you should look at 168 and also the following pages. The same thing is done with statutes by saying *et seq.* at the end of the number, meaning "and so on." For multiple authors, we use *et al.*: "Jones *et al.*"

- *Inter alia* mean "among other things," as in "this statute (legislative act) accomplishes many purposes, *inter alia* the preservation of evidence."

- a *foreign judgment* may refer to an out-of-state one, depending on the context—not necessarily a non-U.S. one. Yes, in this sense California is foreign. *Judgment* in this context means a final, formal decision of a court. Courts may justify their decisions with an *opinion*, often just called a *case*. That's right: the word *case* could mean the entire dispute between parties *or*, confusingly, the written result of it. "I am reading an

---

[4] This chapter is adapted from *Louisiana Notary Exam Sidepiece to the 2021 Study Guide: Tips, Index, Forms—Essentials Missing in the Official Book*, ch. 3 (© 2021).

[5] An excellent, affordable resource for understanding legal vocabulary is also published by Quid Pro Books: Gregory Rome and Stephan Kinsella, *Louisiana Civil Law Dictionary* (2011).

important case that resolved the whole case. So get off my case already."

- Judges along the way may also issue *Orders*. In Louisiana, these tend to be called *Rules*, as used on p. 296 of the study guide. An example: "Judge Diaz issued a Rule to Show Cause today." As a notary, you won't draft proposed Rules for the judge to sign, but you'll often notarize a party's affidavit that supports a proposed Rule. This is different from the "rule" or "holding" that a case sets.

- *Conventional* tends to mean contractual, by agreement, by convention of the parties (like how treaties are called Conventions). In context, it probably doesn't mean "ordinary" or "typical" as it often means in English.

- *Juridical* doesn't mean *judicial*. A judicial act is one done by a court. A juridical act is often done by a notary—not in court—such as a donation.

- *Legal* often means "by operation of law" rather than the opposite of "illegal." A legal mortgage, for example (p. 266), doesn't mean one that isn't forbidden. It means one that arises by law, rather than judicially or conventionally.

- *Special* usually means *specific*, not *super-amazing*. Special interrogatories are a set of questions given to the jury to answer ("Was driver exceeding the speed limit?"), more specific than just "liable" or "not liable." Special damages means specific ones, as opposed to general damages.

- *Interrogatories*, other than in the jury context just noted, are questions given to a party during the pretrial litigation phase called *discovery*, usually in civil cases, not criminal ones. The party then answers the questions under oath (the verification noted at p. 571), which is useful for investigation of the facts and to cross-examine the witness at trial (to "impeach" them if their answers deviate from the pretrial ones).

- *Civil* in one sense refers to the civil law, here meaning Louisiana law, as opposed to the common law derived from England and used in all the other states. But the term *civil* when used to refer to cases or litigation—"the wrongful death case is in civil court"—means that it's not a criminal case. A *civil action* is a private dispute between parties (though sometimes including the government as a party) rather than a charge *by* the government *against* a person for a crime.

- *Authentic* doesn't mean "real," really. It refers to the evidence-law process of *authentication* (identification and verification of its genuineness) that documents have to go though in court to have them "admitted into evidence" and be considered as proof. But in Louisiana *authentic acts* (as well as *acknowledged acts*, both discussed in *Fundamentals* ch. 19) do not need an in-court witness to authenticate them. They can be considered as proof without any witness vouching for them; so they are "self-proving." It doesn't mean the judge or jury has to believe them. But at least the documents are there for their consideration, efficiently produced in court. This creates a role for the Louisiana notary—drafting and verifying documents out-of-court that can then be used in-court without more—that doesn't exist in other states. The authentic act is a civil law wonder.

- *Mandate* may mean a power of attorney (ch. 15 of the study guide). Or, by a court or other legal actor, it can be an order: "This mandate will issue immediately."

- *Parole evidence*, mentioned on study guide pp. 152 and 295, means oral evidence, as opposed to written documentation. There's a real issue in contracts law as to whether parole evidence may be used to deviate from the clear terms of a written contract. But of course there are many situations where it's OK to have an oral contract with no writing whatsoever.

In addition, there are numerous legal terms in the civil law or Louisiana law, discussed in the study guide, that have a meaning quite different from how the word sounds in common parlance. Examples: *naked* owners, *real* rights, and *vulgar* substitutions. Like the above, these are key to know for understanding what you're reading in the study guide. They are potentially testable as well.

ABOUT THE AUTHOR

STEVEN ALAN CHILDRESS is a senior professor at Tulane Law School, holding the Conrad Meyer III Professorship in Civil Procedure. He has taught Torts, Evidence, and Legal Profession at Tulane since 1988, in addition to visiting positions with Loyola–New Orleans and George Washington. He also teaches the Louisiana Notary Law class in Tulane's School of Professional Advancement. He has lectured for 'continuing legal education' on notary practice, legal ethics, and evidence law, as well as teaching Louisiana Bar Review for a decade.

Alan earned his law degree from Harvard and a PhD in Jurisprudence from Berkeley. He clerked in Shreveport for the federal court of appeals, then practiced law in California with two national firms. He is a member of the Louisiana Notary Association, the Law & Society Association, and the California and D.C. bar associations. He's in the relatively rare posture of having taken both a bar exam and the state notarial exam. He coauthored the three-volume treatise *Federal Standards of Review*, edited three books on legal ethics, and annotated a 2010 edition of Oliver Wendell Holmes's *The Common Law*. Recently, he published the best-selling prep resource *Louisiana Notary Exam Sidepiece to the 2021 Study Guide,* as well as *Louisiana Notary Exam Sample Questions and Answers 2021.*

He is a commissioned Louisiana notary public who, with his wife Michele (an attorney-notary since 2002), has owned and operated a notary/shipping service in Jefferson Parish. They have performed thousands of notarial acts covering a wide range of subjects and formats. Alan is also a practicing notary for the Tulane University community. He may be contacted at *achildress@tulane.edu.*

qp
QUID PRO BOOKS

Visit us at *www.quidprobooks.com.*

www.ingramcontent.com/pod-product-compliance
Lightning Source LLC
Chambersburg PA
CBHW081041110426
42740CB00051B/3137